X-TREME FACTS: U.S. HISTORY

THE WHITE HOUSE

by Campbell Collison

BEARPORT PUBLISHING

Minneapolis, Minnesota

Credits:

© Cover, clockwise from bottom left, John Trumbull/Public Domain; Nerthuz/Shutterstock; George Peter Alexander Healy/Public Domain; imagedj/Shutterstock; Title Page, Orhan Cam/Shutterstock; 4, Everett Historical/Shutterstock.com; 5 top, George Munger/Public Domain; 5 right, Bass Otis/Public Domain; 5 middle, Library of Congress/Public Domain; 5 left, David P. Lewis/Shutterstock.com; 6 top, James Hoban/Public Domain; 6 left, John Christian Rauschner/Public Domain; 6 right, John Trumbull/Public Domain; 7 top, George Cooke/Public Domain; 7, .E. Walker/Public Domain; 7 left, right, Gilbert Stuart/Public Domain; 8 bottom background Joraca/Shutterstock; 8 bottom left, 8-29 Austen Photography; 8 top, Suzanne Tucker/Shutterstock; 8 right, LightField Studios/Shutterstock; 9 top, The White House/Public Domain; 9 left, Nationaal Archief/Creative Commons; 9 right, (Mr) Smith, War Office official photographer/Public Domain; 9 bottom background, AudeVivere/Creative Commons;10 top, Executive Office of the President of the United States/Public Domain; 10, LightField Studios/Shutterstock; 11 top, Ritu Manoj Jethani/Shutterstock.com; 11 middle, Sashkin/Shutterstock; 11, Executive Office of the President of the United States/Public Domain; 12 top, Carol M. Highsmith/General Services Administration/Public Domain; 12, Leika production/Shutterstock; 13 top, Annie Leibovitz/Released by White House Photo Office/Public Domain; 13 middle, Official White House Photo by Chuck Kennedy/Public Domain; 13 bottom, padmak/Shutterstock.com; 13 right, Everett Historical/Shutterstock; 14, Bumble Dee/Shutterstock.com; 14 right, Chernetskaya/Dreamstime.com; 15 top, 15 bottom, 27, Pete Souza, Executive Office of the President of the United State/Public Domain; 15 middle, Ronald Regan Archives/Public Domain; 16, Executive Office of the President of the United States/Public Domain; 17 top, 1000 Words/Shutterstock.com; 17 right, Records of the White House Photo Office/Public Domain; 17 left, Viorel Sima/Shutterstock; 17, Orhan Cam/Shutterstock; 18 top, Everett Historical/Shutterstock; 18, The U.S. National Archives/Public Domain; 19 top, Orhan Cam/Shutterstock; 19 top left, bottom left, 21 bottom middle, LightField Studios/Shutterstock; 19 top right, Nicole Glass Photography/Shutterstock.com; 19 bottom right, Gage Skidmore/Creative Commons; 20 top, Joseph Sohm/Shutterstock.com; 20 right, Harriet Anderson Stubbs Murphy/Public Domain; 21 top, 360b/Shutterstock.com; 21 bottom left, Roman Tiraspolsky/Shutterstock.com; 21 bottom right, Roman Tiraspolsky/Shutterstock.com; 22 top, U.S. Navy photo by Photographer's Mate 2nd Class Daniel J. McLain/Public Domain; 22 bottom, Executive Office of the President of the United States/Public Domain; 23 top, DoD photo by U.S. Air Force Staff Sgt. Marianique Santos/Public Domain; 23 bottom, Official White House Photo by Joyce N. Boghosian/Public Domain; 23 bottom left, Gelpi/Shutterstock; 23 bottom right, Anna Om/Shutterstock; 24 top, The White House. Samantha Appleton, photographer/Public Domain; 24 left, Nik Merkulov/Shutterstock; 24 right, Gift; Michael Geissinger, photographer/Public Domain; 25 top, Official White House Photo by D. Myles Cullen/Public Domain; 25 middle, Brian A Jackson/Shutterstock; 25 bottom left, VGstockstudio/Shutterstock; 25 bottom right, White House Photographic Office/Public Domain; 26 top left, Anders Zorn/Public Domain; 26 top right, Anders Zorn/Public Domain; 26, Official White House Photo by Joyce N. Boghosian)/Public Domain; 26 bottom right, StockImageFactory.com/Shutterstock; 27 top, U.S. Government/White House photo by Kimberlee Hewitt/Public Domain; 27 middle, Daniel Huntington/Public Domain; 27 bottom New Africa/Shutterstock; 28 top, Luca Perra/Shutterstock; 28 bottom middle, Oleksandr Lytvynenko/Shutterstock; 28 bottom right, koya979/Shutterstock; 29 bottom left, Ivan Kokoulin/Dreamstime.com; 28-29, Austen Photography

Developed and produced for Bearport Publishing by BlueAppleWorks Inc.
Managing Editor for BlueAppleWorks: Melissa McClellan
Art Director: T.J. Choleva
Photo Research: Jane Reid
Editor: Marcia Abramson

Library of Congress Cataloging-in-Publication Data

Names: Collison, Campbell, author.
Title: The White House / by Campbell Collison.
Description: Minneapolis, MN : Bearport Publishing Company, [2021] | Series: Xtreme facts: U.S. history | Includes bibliographical references and index.
Identifiers: LCCN 2020012917 | ISBN 9781647471231 (library binding) | ISBN 9781647471309 (paperback) | ISBN 9781647471378 (ebook)
Subjects: LCSH: White House (Washington, D.C.)—Juvenile literature. | Washington (D.C.)—Buildings, structures, etc.—Juvenile literature. | Presidents—United States—Juvenile literature.
Classification: LCC F204.W5 C63 2021 | DDC 975.3—dc23
LC record available at https://lccn.loc.gov/2020012917

For more information, write to Bearport Publishing, 5357 Penn Avenue South, Minneapolis, MN 55419.
Printed in the United States of America.

Contents

The White House Is Burning!

Just over 30 years after the end of the American Revolution, British forces were back in the United States waging war. The British troops had entered Washington, D.C. and were destroying the still-new capital city. As the British approached the White House, they learned President James Madison had already fled. Though disappointed, the soldiers raided the kitchen and stole what they could. Then, they set the White House on fire!

The War of 1812 was fought over British military interference in U.S. trade.

The War of 1812 is often called the Second Revolution. The fighting lasted from June of 1812 until February of 1815.

Heavy rain and one or more tornadoes dampened the fires and **halted the British attack on Washington**, D.C.

By the end of the attack in 1814, only the burnt shell of the White House remained. But by October 1817, the rebuilt White House was ready for President James Monroe to move in.

The White House has been known as the President's Palace, the President's House, and the **Executive** Mansion. **President Theodore Roosevelt officially gave the White House its current name in 1901.**

First Lady Dolley Madison left personal belongings behind during the British invasion and told the **White House staff to save a portrait of George Washington instead.**

Building a Capital City

When the U.S. Constitution called for a new national capital, Congress decided it would be built along the banks of the Potomac River on land that was originally part of Maryland and Virginia. But it was up to President George Washington to decide the details for the president's house. Washington picked a location and held a competition for the building's design. **Architect** James Hoban's plan won.

A 1793 sketch shows Hoban's vision for the White House.

President George Washington oversaw the building of the residence, but he never actually lived there.

The White House is only a couple of miles (about 4 km) from the U.S. Capitol Building.

Washington, D.C., is built along the riverbank.

Second President John Adams and First Lady Abigail Adams were the first to live in the White House. When they moved in, only six rooms were finished.

President Adams wrote about the White House in a letter to his wife. He said, "May none but honest and wise men ever rule under this roof."

The Haunted White House?

The White House is an old mansion packed with history, so it's no surprise that some people believe it's haunted. Presidents, First Ladies, staff members, and guests have reported feeling spooky presences, hearing unexplained noises, and even running into actual ghosts. The ghost of President Abraham Lincoln is the most commonly reported sighting.

An unnamed British soldier who died during the War of 1812 is said to roam **the White House grounds.**

William Henry Harrison, the first president to die in the White House, **is said to haunt the attic.**

Jenna Bush Hager, daughter of President George W. Bush, once heard piano music coming from her bedroom's fireplace.

Ghosts and goblins have been decorating the White House for Halloween since 1958.

Queen Wilhelmina, visiting from the Netherlands, answered a knock on her bedroom door and **saw Lincoln's ghost**. She fainted on the spot!

As he was getting out of a bathtub, British Prime Minister **Winston Churchill saw the ghost of Lincoln, too.**

A White House Tour

The White House has always been a work in progress. It has been rebuilt, expanded, and renovated through the years to give each president the best workplace and home possible. The White House has three main parts. The West Wing contains the Oval Office where the president and senior staff work. The East Wing has the visitor's entrance and staff offices for the First Lady or First Gentleman. The Executive Residence, where the First Family lives, is in the middle of the building.

The White House has 132 rooms, 147 windows, 35 bathrooms, 28 fireplaces, 8 staircases, and 3 elevators.

Official government events are held on the first floor of the White House.

The White House contains a chocolate shop, a flower shop, a music room, and a map room.

First Lady Pat Nixon made the White House wheelchair-friendly for public tours. She also designed tours for people who are blind and those with hearing loss.

White House tours are very popular. They need to be booked months in advance.

The **White House** has a swimming pool, a gym, a movie theater, a game room, and a bowling alley.

The First Family can see any movie they want at any time of the day in their very own movie theater!

President Barack Obama invited guests to watch *Men in Black 3*. They were even given 3D glasses!

Moving Day for the President

January 20 is the **inauguration** day of the new president and also the moving day for the old one! The old and new president meet at the White House in the morning and then travel together to the inauguration. The moving trucks for both families arrive at about 11 a.m. By the time the new First Family returns from the ceremony and parade, most of the move is completed.

The incoming president spends the night before the inauguration at the nearby guesthouse called **Blair House**.

Blair House is made of four historic row houses that were connected together.

The First Families, both incoming and outgoing, **are responsible for paying the moving costs**.

When First Daughters Sasha and Malia Obama moved into the White House, they found a welcome letter from First Daughters Barbara and Jenna Bush.

The Obamas arranged for Malia and Sasha to tour the White House before moving day so they would feel at home.

The White House staff clean windows, vacuum carpets, and hang photos for the incoming president.

When **President George Washington** left office, he **only needed a couple of wagons to carry his papers** to his home at Mount Vernon, Virginia.

Meet the Staff

The White House is both a huge mansion and a massive office building. So it's no wonder that about 90 full-time staff members are needed to keep it running smoothly. First among them is the chief **usher** who oversees the day-to-day management of the White House residence and staff. Staff members include doormen, butlers, maids, housekeepers, chefs, florists, carpenters, plumbers, and electricians.

In addition to the full-time staff, **the White House has about 250 part-time employees.**

President Obama hired the first female chief usher. Her name was Angella Reid.

The White House has a full-time pastry chef who creates desserts and treats for the First Family and for important functions like **state dinners**.

Susie Morrison celebrated becoming the first female executive pastry chef with a fist bump from President Barack Obama in the White House kitchen.

Presidents pay for all their personal expenses, including toiletries, clothing, and dry cleaning.

Eugene Allen served as a pantry man, butler, and **maitre d'** over his 34 years at the White House. He worked for eight presidents.

More than 70,000 bees live in the White House's Kitchen Garden. A beekeeper harvests honey for the First Family and their guests.

White House Rules

Every home has its rules, but the White House has some extra ones. After all, it's a house that belongs to the entire nation! All changes to White House rooms and grounds must be approved. In addition, a president must follow traditional rules during formal activities, such as when hosting formal dinners. Few presidents have complained about the rules, but President Harry Truman once referred to the White House as "the great white jail."

President George H. W. Bush and First Lady Barbara Bush made their own Sunday dinners so their kitchen staff could have some time off.

The children of presidents can pick the decorations for their bedrooms.

White House events follow rules known as protocol. The Chief of Protocol helps the president and the staff make sure that guests are not offended or embarrassed.

For safety reasons, presidents are not allowed to drive a car on public roads!

Presidents ride in an armored car called the Beast!

President George W. Bush's daughters **Jenna and Barbara** liked to slide down the **banisters** of the White House staircases.

Windows in the White House are sealed shut.

The Wired White House

In 1877, when President Rutherford B. Hayes had the first telephone put into the White House, the phone number was simply 1! But the phone was tucked away in a small office called the **Telegraph** Room. It wasn't until 1929 that President Herbert Hoover installed a phone on his desk in the Oval Office. Barack Obama was the first president to be allowed to use a smartphone. The White House has been slow to adapt to the use of smartphone technology and social media because of fears about hacking and spying.

In 1902, the Telegraph Room became a sitting room next to a bedroom that was once President Lincoln's office. Today, they are known as the Lincoln Bedroom and Sitting Room.

President Bill Clinton launched the first ever White House website. With each new administration, the website is redesigned.

President Donald Trump is a big fan of Twitter. He has sent out more than 100 tweets in a single day!

A communications director, press secretary, and dozens of staffers help the president get his message across.

For security reasons, President Barack Obama's smartphone couldn't text or take pictures.

First Lady Michelle Obama didn't let her daughters **Sasha and Malia Obama** use Twitter.

To Serve and Protect

The U.S. Secret Service is not so secret. They are always protecting the president's family, the vice president's family, and former presidents. The Secret Service secures any area the president will be visiting or passing through. Being watched constantly isn't easy. Agents even follow presidents into the bathroom! Even President Barack Obama's pickup basketball games on the White House court had to be supervised by Secret Service agents.

Secret Service agents are expected to do anything necessary to keep members of the First Family safe.

More than 6,500 men and women serve as Secret Service agents.

The Secret Service began protecting presidents in 1901 after President William McKinley was killed.

Each member of the First Family is given a code name by the Secret Service. President Obama was Renegade, First Lady Michelle Obama was Renaissance, and their daughters Malia and Sasha were Radiance and Rosebud.

Agents wear earpieces and hidden microphones to keep in touch.

Agents escort the president's children to school each day. First Kids are protected until they are at least 16, even if their parents are no longer in the White House.

The President Takes to the Skies

Presidents need to think fast and move faster. From crisscrossing the country to speak with fellow Americans to jetting around the globe for meetings with world leaders, presidents rely on their special airplane known as Air Force One. And if a president needs a quick local getaway or wants to avoid traffic jams when getting to the airport, hopping on the Marine One helicopter is the way to go.

In 1943, Franklin Roosevelt was the first president to use an airplane on official business.

Following President John F. Kennedy's **assassination** in 1963, **Vice President Lyndon B. Johnson took the presidential oath on Air Force One.**

The name Air Force One is used for any air force aircraft carrying the president.

A temporary landing and takeoff site is set up on the White House lawn for Marine One.

President Barack Obama joked that getting rides on Marine One was the presidential perk he would miss most.

It's a tradition for the outgoing president to leave office on Marine One, as President Obama did in 2017.

For security purposes, **Marine One always flies in a group of up to five identical helicopters.**

On July 16, 2009, **the first all-female Marine One crew flew President Obama from the White House** to Andrews Air Force Base in Maryland.

What's Cooking?

From whipping up simple meals and snacks to preparing fancy state dinners, the White House chefs can do it all. With that much cooking, more than one kitchen is needed. A small kitchen serves most of the everyday meals for the First Family. There's also a main kitchen that serves the bigger meals and a pastry kitchen just for making desserts. A team of at least five full-time chefs **cater** to every presidential taste.

Cristeta Comerford, an immigrant from the Philippines, became the first female White House executive chef in 2005.

Comerford had a staff of about 30 chefs, cooks, and helpers.

President George H. W. Bush famously declared he would no longer eat broccoli.

The State Dining Room can seat 140 guests for dinner. If only appetizers are on the menu, as many as 1,000 people can be served.

The White House aims to please! Burgers and fries were served when President Donald Trump hosted the North Dakota Bisons to celebrate their 2019 college football championship.

Want a soda or a snack? Just press the button on the Oval Office desk, and it will be there in no time!

President Ronald Reagan had more than 700 bags of jelly beans delivered to the White House every month. He shared them with staff and visitors.

Presidents pay for all of their groceries. The government pays for the chefs and kitchen staff.

Holidays at the White House

When it comes to holidays, the White House shares the celebrations with the entire nation. In 1889, President Benjamin Harrison put up the first Christmas tree at the White House. White House tradition now calls for dozens of trees, inside and out, and thousands of decorative lights. Today, White House celebrations include Christmas, Hanukkah, Diwali, Ramadan, and other holidays important to Americans across the country.

In 1895, **President Grover Cleveland and First Lady Frances Cleveland** put up the first Christmas tree that was decorated with electric lights.

The National Christmas Tree grows in a park by the White House.

In 2009, **President Barack Obama** became the first president to celebrate Diwali at the White House.

President Jimmy Carter was the first president to light a large outdoor **Hanukkah menorah**.

President George W. Bush was the first president to light a menorah inside the White House.

Real eggs are used in the White House Easter Egg Roll. In 2019, egg farmers donated 74,000 eggs for the event!

The White House Easter Egg Roll tradition began in 1878 with President Rutherford B. Hayes.

House-in-a-Box
CRAFT PROJECT

Dioramas are **three-dimensional** (3D) scenes inside a frame. They are used to tell a story or capture a moment in time. Make your own White House diorama! Be sure to grab a deep box so it can have a background, middle ground, and foreground.

Over 4,000 tulips bloom each spring around the circular pool and fountain in front of **the White House!**

What You Will Need

- A deep box
- Construction paper in white, blue, green, and brown
- Scissors
- Glue and tape
- White posterboard
- Tissue paper in red, blue, and green
- Markers
- A toothpick

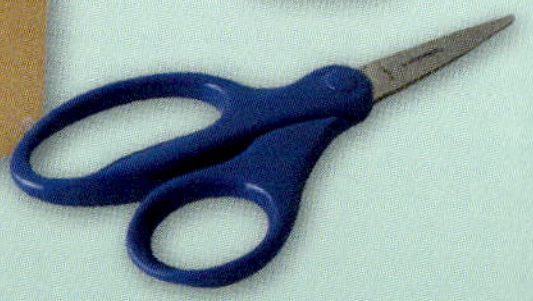

Step One

Cut and glue pieces of blue construction paper to the walls of your box for sky. Do the same with green construction paper on the bottom for grass.

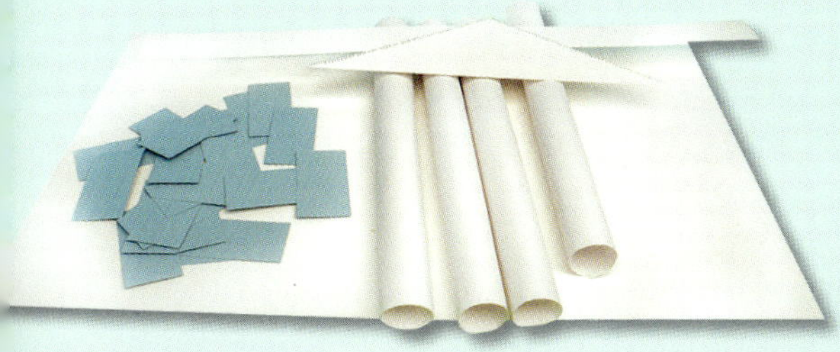

Step Two

Cut a large rectangle, a triangle, and a long slim rectangle out of white posterboard for the building and roof. Cut 22 small rectangles out of blue construction paper for the windows. Cut four pieces of white construction paper the same height as the large rectangle. Roll them up to make columns. Glue or tape all the pieces in place.

Step Three

Roll up two pieces of brown construction paper for tree trunks. Crumple up green tissue paper for treetops and shrubs. Crumple up red tissue paper for flowers and blue for the fountain. Glue or tape everything in place. Cut a small rectangle of white construction paper and color it as an American flag. Tape it to a toothpick, and tape the toothpick to the roof.

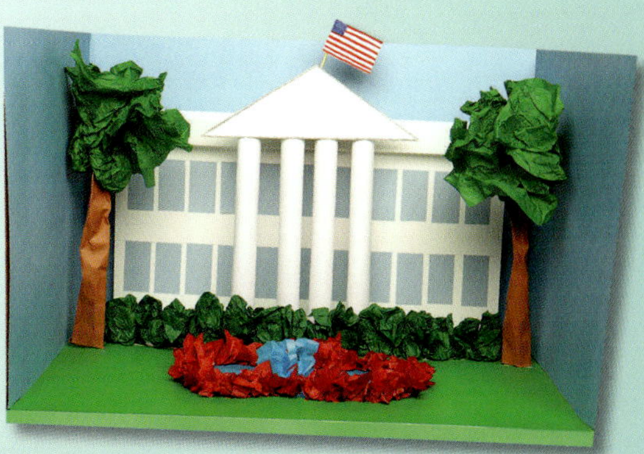

The back of the White House faces the South Lawn.

Glossary

architect a person who designs buildings and prepares detailed plans for builders to use

assassination the murder of a public person or political leader

banister the railing of a staircase

cater to provide what people want

diorama a three-dimensional model of a scene

executive related to the branch of government that includes the president and vice president

inauguration the swearing-in ceremony that marks the beginning of a president's term of office

maitre d' the person at a restaurant or formal dining room who directs the waiters and kitchen staff

state dinner a formal dinner, usually hosting a foreign diplomat or leader from another nation

telegraph a device that sends messages over long distances by electrical wires

three-dimensional having height, length, and depth

usher the person who directs the household staff

Read More

Arnold, Tedd. *Fly Guy Presents: The White House (Fly Guy Presents Scholastic Reader Level 2).* New York: Scholastic (2016).

Collison, Campbell. *The Presidents (X-Treme Facts: U.S. History).* Minneapolis: Bearport (2021).

Stine, Megan. *Where Is the White House?* New York: Grosset & Dunlap (2015).

Learn More Online

1. Go to **www.factsurfer.com**
2. Enter "**White House**" into the search box.
3. Click on the cover of this book to see a list of websites.

Index

About the Author

Campbell Collison is the pseudonym for Cathy Collison and Janis Campbell. The two Michigan writers are both married and have two grown children each. They are avid history tourists and love uncovering fun facts, whether traveling to historic homes, presidential libraries, or national parks across the country. The friends have been writing partners for 25 years.